MAKING **HISTORY**

WORLD WAR II

Rupert Matthews and Sue Nicholson

W
FRANKLIN WATTS
LONDON•SYDNEY

First published in 2008 by Franklin Watts

Copyright © Franklin Watts 2008

Franklin Watts
338 Euston Road
London NW1 3BH

Franklin Watts Australia
Level 17/207 Kent Street
Sydney, NSW 2000

A CIP catalogue record for this book is available
from the British Library.

Created by Q2AMedia
Editor: Jean Coppendale
Creative Director: Simmi Sikka

ISBN 978 0 7496 7853 1

Note to parents and teachers:
Every effort has been made by the Publisher to ensure that the websites in this book are suitable for children, that they
are of the highest educational value, and that they contain no inappropriate or offensive material. However, because of the nature
of the Internet, it is impossible to guarantee that the contents of these sites will not be altered. We strongly advise that Internet
access is supervised by a responsible adult.

Many projects in this book require adult supervision, especially those which involve the use
of scissors and craft knives. Some projects suggest the use of wallpaper paste. It is advised that a fungicide-free
paste (cellulose paste) is used. If in doubt, consult the manufacturer's contents list and instructions. Many projects suggest
the use of paint. It is advised that non-toxic paint is used. If in doubt, consult the manufacturer's contents list and instructions.

Picture Credits:
Cover: Q2AMedia
t: top, b: bottom, m: middle, c: centre, l: left, r: right
4 : Popperfoto/Getty Images ; 5t : Bettmann/CORBIS ; 5b : ASSOCIATED PRESS ; 6t : Time & Life Pictures/Getty Images ; 6b : The National Archives ;
7t : ASSOCIATED PRESS ; 8tl : Imperial War Museum ; 8br : Maeers/ Getty Images ; 10tr : Imperial War Museum ; 10br : The National Archives ;
11t, 11b : ASSOCIATED PRESS ; 12tr : Daniel Boiteau/ Dreamstime ; 12 bl : NASA ; 12 br : Canadian Warplane Heritage Museum ; 14t : Mary Evans
Picture Library/ Photolibrary ; 14b : ASSOCIATED PRESS ; 15 : ASSOCIATED PRESS ; 16 : WW2 In Color ; 18tr : ASSOCIATED PRESS ; 18bl : Imperial
War Museum ; 20tr : Popperfoto/Getty Images ; 20bl : Time & Life Pictures/Getty Images ; 20br : The National Archives ; 21tr, 21ml : Gregory Davies /
Alamy ; 22tr : Magnus Manske ; 23t : The National Archives ; 23b : New Zealand Defense Force ; 24bl : The National Archives ; 26 : DOD Media ; 27t,
27b : The National Archives ; 28bl : Popperfoto/Getty Images ; 28br : Shylov Victor Evgenevich/ Shutterstock.

Printed in China

Franklin Watts is a division of Hachette Children's Books, an Hachette Livre UK company.
www.hachettelivre.co.uk

Contents

The World at War

World War II began in September 1939, when the armed forces of Nazi Germany invaded Poland. By the time the war ended in 1945, millions had died and whole countries lay in ruins.

Global conflict

World War II was really a series of wars that merged into one. On one side were the Axis powers of Germany, Italy and Japan. Opposing them were Great Britain and, later, the US and Soviet Russia.

After Nazi dictator Adolf Hitler invaded Poland, Great Britain and France declared war on Germany. Polish soldiers and airmen fled to England to carry on fighting the Germans. As the conflict spread, more and more countries became drawn in. By the end of the war almost every country in the world was involved.

1939: Countdown to War

29 August British Ambassador flies to Berlin for crisis talks with the German dictator, Adolf Hitler. In Polish city of Danzig, Nazis attack shops and smash windows.

30 August British government repeats earlier promise to support Poland if country is attacked by Germany.

31 August Germany announces 16-point plan for settlement of Polish crisis.

1 September Germany invades Poland. Warsaw and other cities bombed.

2 September Emergency meeting of British parliament. Prime Minister Chamberlain threatens to go to war with Germany unless troops removed from Polish soil.

3 September Deadline for withdrawal of German troops expires. Britain declares war on Germany. King George VI broadcasts to nation. In London the first air-raid warning turns out to be a false alarm.

◄ During the war the British leader Winston Churchill (1874–1965) made many famous speeches urging people to stand firm against Hitler. In the 1930s, Churchill had often tried to warn people about the growing threat from Nazi Germany.

On 7 December 1941, Japanese planes bombed the American naval base at Pearl Harbor. Many ships and aircraft were destroyed and more than 2,000 US servicemen lost their lives. Before the attack, many Americans believed their country should stay out of the war. Afterwards, America declared war on Japan and joined the Allied side.

What caused World War II?

After Germany's defeat in World War I (1914–18), Adolf Hitler wanted to make his country strong again. Under his rule, the Nazi party became all-powerful. Businesses owned by Jews and foreigners were seized. Hitler also rearmed Germany with huge forces of tanks and planes and threatened to invade neighbouring countries.

Some countries believed they could avoid war by making deals with Hitler. But when German troops invaded Poland in 1939, Hitler showed his real intentions.

◀ The Nazi leader Adolf Hitler (1889–1945) ruled Germany from 1933. His extreme policies and racist ideas led directly to war and to the mass-murder of millions of European Jews.

Blitzkrieg!

In 1940, Nazi armies swept across Europe. German bombers pounded towns and cities. Tanks and soldiers quickly seized control of key positions. This type of fighting was called Blitzkrieg or 'lightning war'.

The fall of Europe

German troops conquered Poland in just four weeks. Soon afterwards, Hitler's Russian allies attacked Finland, and Germany invaded Denmark and Norway.

In May 1940, Hitler launched devastating attacks on the Netherlands, Belgium and France. One by one, the countries fell into German hands. By August, Hitler's armies had overrun most of mainland Europe. Now only Britain held out against the Nazis.

▲ Surprise bombing raids by German planes caught defenders off guard. While civilians fled in panic, German troops and tanks stormed into action.

◀ Victorious German troops march through the streets of Warsaw. Poland's poorly equipped army was no match for these highly trained and disciplined soldiers.

▲ Tanks were a vital part of Hitler's Blitzkrieg tactics. Light, fast-moving tanks such as these Panzer MKII raced ahead of the soldiers to scout the ground and capture key bridges. The heaver Panzer MKIV with its big gun was brought up to deal with any tough resistance.

The 'Phoney War'

When war was first declared, people in Britain and France expected the Germans to attack them straight away – but instead there were several months of anxious waiting. The British called this time the 'Phoney War'.

Food rationing

One of the first worries was food. In January 1940, rationing was brought in to make sure that foods that were scarce were shared out fairly.

On the defensive

In London, important buildings such as the Houses of Parliament were protected with barbed wire and sandbags.

In the countryside, road signs were taken down to confuse enemy troops in case of an invasion. More than a million men who were too young or old to be regular soldiers joined local defence units. These later became known as the Home Guard.

Food Rationing

During the war, Britain's farmers could not grow enough to feed everybody, so the government brought in rationing to make sure there were fair shares for all. At first only butter, sugar and bacon were rationed. As the war went on, the list of rationed foods grew longer. Every Sunday evening people listened to a special radio broadcast telling them which goods would be rationed that week.

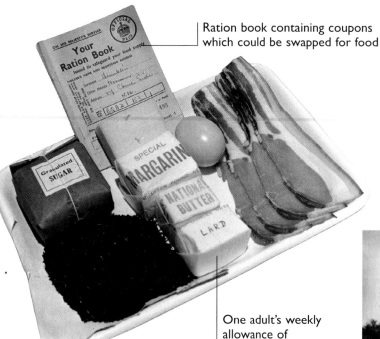

Ration book containing coupons which could be swapped for food

One adult's weekly allowance of rationed foods

▲ When a customer bought food, the shopkeeper tore out a coupon from their ration book to show that the week's ration had been bought. As well as basic rations, everyone was allowed 16 points a month to spend as they liked. The picture shows one adult's weekly amount of rationed foods in August 1942.

How to play

You have just been given your ration book from the Ministry of Food. Now it is time to play the rationing game!

You will need a counter for each player, and a dice.

Take turns to roll the dice. Move your counter according the number on the dice, and follow the instructions on the squares.

The winner is the first person to reach the last square.

▲ To help grow more food, many women joined the Women's Land Army. Farm work was hard, and the women did all sorts of jobs, including hoeing and ploughing, hay-making and looking after farm animals.

PLAY

THE RATIONING GAME

Go back 1 space.

Butcher has run out of meat.

Move on 3 spaces.

Make old curtains into clothing.

Roll again.

Ham for Christmas lunch!

Go back 4 spaces.

queues at grocer's.

Long

Win

Well done – you have made it!

Get an allotment to grow more vegetables and fruit. **Roll again.**

July 1942 Sweets and chocolate rationed. *Miss a turn.*

February 1942 Soap rationed to one small tablet a month. *Move back 3 spaces.*

Rip Rip hole in clothes. *Miss 1 turn.*

Start to keep chickens for eggs. *Move on 5 spaces.*

Help to feed pigs kept in rubble of bombed houses nearby. *Move on 1 space.*

Loss Lose ration book! *Go back to START.*

Bumper crop of carrots, onions and potatoes! *Move on 3 spaces.*

June 1941 Limited to one fresh egg a week – no eggs at grocers! *Go back 2 spaces.*

June 1941 Clothes rationing starts. *Go back 1 space.*

RATIONING GAME

January 1940

START ➡

Queue up for your first rations of bacon, ham, sugar and butter. *Miss 1 turn.*

July 1940 Sugar ration cut. *Move back 1 space.*

Government announces no fresh or tinned fruit to be imported, except oranges for children. *Miss 1 turn.*

Dig up roses to make room for carrots and onions instead. *Move on 2 spaces.*

Swap coupons to get extra sugar and butter to make birthday cake. *Throw again.*

War in the Air

After the fall of France, Hitler's plan was to launch a huge invasion of Britain across the English Channel, codenamed 'Operation Sealion'. But first, German planes had to win control of the air.

The 'Battle of Britain'

Between 10 July and 31 October 1940, Britain's Royal Air Force (RAF) fought a fierce battle against the Germany's Luftwaffe in the skies over southern England. Day after day, RAF planes such as Hurricanes and Spitfires took to the air to defend Britain against German bomber planes and Messerschmitt fighters.

The RAF pilots were heavily outnumbered, but shot down 1,368 enemy aircraft and lost only 832 planes of their own. It was a narrow but crucial victory for the Allies. After this, Hitler gave up his plans to invade Britain.

▲ During the war, the British used a system called radar (radio detection and ranging) to spot enemy aircraft and plot their speed and direction. These men and women are working in an RAF radar receiving station during the Battle of Britain.

▶ On a London rooftop, an air-raid warden scans the skies for signs of enemy aircraft.

◀ During the war, Churchill directed operations from this underground room in London's Whitehall. The room was heavily fortified so that work could carry on through German air raids.

▲ German planes head for targets in the South of England. At the start of the conflict, the Luftwaffe had many well trained and experienced pilots, but the RAF pilots were skilled, determined and well organised. In the air, the German planes were often an easy target for the more agile RAF Spitfires.

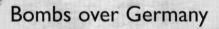

Bombs over Germany

World War II was the first war in which aircraft played an important part. At first German planes controlled the skies. But soon the Allies began to fight back.

After May 1940, RAF bombers started to hit key targets in Germany. From 1942, bombing raids by RAF and US planes became a vital part of the Allies' plan to win the war.

Two RAF Mosquito fighter-bombers in ▶ flight after a daylight raid on Berlin, Germany, in January 1943.

Planes of World War II

The Battle of Britain was the first major conflict ever to be fought and won in the air. RAF Spitfires played a crucial part in the Allied victory. They were much loved by their pilots and saw service throughout the war.

This project shows you how to make World War II planes out of modelling clay.

Spitfire

Fast and agile, the Spitfire was the best RAF fighter plane of the war. The German pilots feared the Spitfire and did their best to destroy the factories where the planes were built.

Stuka

The German Stuka dive bomber could drop a 500 kg bomb on to a target as small as a single house. A siren fixed to its wheels made a terrifying noise as it dived to drop its bombs.

Mustang

The long-range single-seat US Mustang fighter flew many bomber escort missions over Germany. Mustangs also saw action against the Japanese during the war in the Pacific.

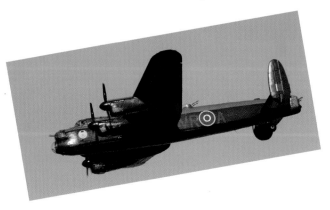

Lancaster

The four-engine Lancaster was one of the RAF's main heavy bombers and was often used for nighttime raids. It became famous in the 1943 'Dam Buster' raids on Germany's Ruhr Valley dams.

You will need

- Self-hardening modelling clay
- Cocktail sticks
- Paints
- Paintbrush

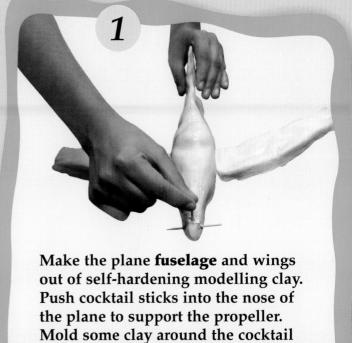

1

Make the plane **fuselage** and wings out of self-hardening modelling clay. Push cocktail sticks into the nose of the plane to support the propeller. Mold some clay around the cocktail sticks to make the propeller blades.

2

When dry, paint your planes in camouflage colours. Don't forget to add markings, such as the American star or the RAF roundel (see Spitfire opposite).

The Home Front

World War II affected more people than any other war. In Britain, the term 'Home Front' was used to show that people at home were taking part just as much as the fighting soldiers.

The Blitz

After giving up his invasion plans, Hitler tried to defeat Britain slowly. His plan now was to destroy towns and cities from the air and shatter civilian morale. This time was called the Blitz. The bombing raids reached a peak in the summer of 1941, but continued until 1944.

London and other cities were bombed night after night. About 40,000 people were killed and 50,000 injured. After 1942, the RAF began to hit back with huge bombing raids on German cities.

▲ This famous picture of St Paul's Cathedral was taken during one of the worst raids of the Blitz. In spite of the heavy death toll, Britain did not surrender as Hitler had hoped.

◄ Rescue workers remove a body from the wreckage of a house bombed in a German air raid. During the Blitz, wardens and fire-fighters often risked their lives rescuing people trapped in blazing buildings.

▲ When war began, London had its own ready-made air-raid shelter system – the Underground. At the peak of the Blitz, as many as 177,000 Londoners flocked to the Underground stations to escape the falling bombs.

Living through the Blitz

Despite the bombing, ordinary people tried to get on with life as best they could. But food and other goods were scarce. Everybody had to work very hard to support the war effort.

Evacuees

In the autumn of 1939, many children were evacuated from the cities to the country. Children and adults were given gas masks to carry with them at all times in case German planes dropped canisters of poison gas.

Air-raid shelters

When an air-raid siren sounded, people ran to the nearest shelter and stayed until they heard the 'all-clear'. Some homes had a shelter in the back garden. Shelters saved many lives, but they could not protect the people inside against a direct hit.

Any old iron?

All sorts of materials were in short supply during the war, especially metals. Many people gave their spare saucepans and iron railings to be turned into guns and aircraft parts.

A Child's War

Being evacuated to the country gave many children their first chance to see green fields and farm animals. Some liked it. Others missed their family and felt very homesick. Children who stayed in the cities got used to playing in rubble-filled streets and bomb sites. Sweets were rationed, and there were few toys and clothes to buy in the shops.

To help families cope with shortages, the government launched a 'Make Do and Mend' campaign. This project shows you how to make a child's toy from scraps of fabric and wool.

▲ During the war toys and games were in short supply, but children could still have fun dressing up and playing soldiers.

1

Fold the fabric in half, right sides facing, and pin the sides together. Draw a doll shape on the fabric, adding an extra 1 cm all round.

4

Glue on wool for the doll's hair. Add features with a felt-tip pen, and make some simple doll's clothes from fabric scraps. Cut the fabric with pinking shears so the edges do not fray and glue the sides together.

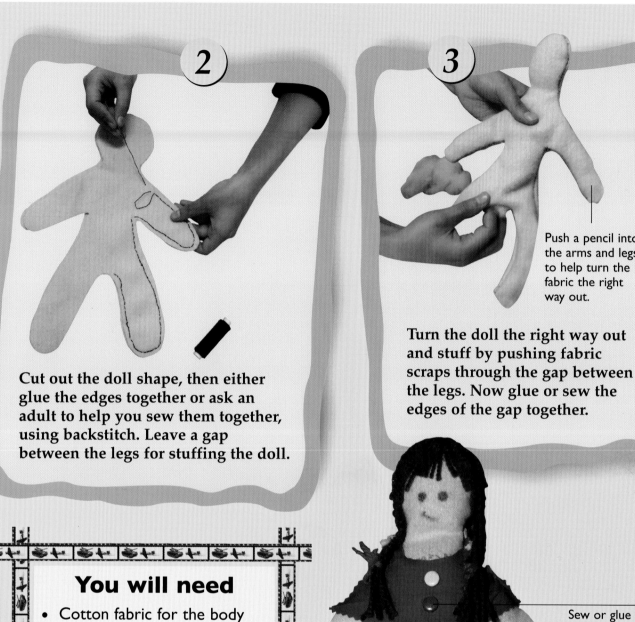

2

Cut out the doll shape, then either glue the edges together or ask an adult to help you sew them together, using backstitch. Leave a gap between the legs for stuffing the doll.

3

Push a pencil into the arms and legs to help turn the fabric the right way out.

Turn the doll the right way out and stuff by pushing fabric scraps through the gap between the legs. Now glue or sew the edges of the gap together.

You will need

- Cotton fabric for the body
- Pins
- Scissors and pinking shears
- Needle and thread
- Fabric glue
- Felt-tip pen
- Wool for the doll's hair
- Scraps of patterned fabric for doll's clothes

Sew or glue on buttons or braid to decorate dress.

Glue edges of dress together at sides

The War at Sea

While home-grown food was scarce, the British relied on ships to bring in supplies by sea. The Germans hoped that by sinking the supply ships, they could starve the British out and force them to surrender.

The U-boat threat

The German Navy used U-boats (submarines) to attack ships bringing food and other supplies to Britain. Each U-boat had a gun for use on the surface and 23 torpedoes. The U-boats usually stayed below the surface during the day, then came up to attack the ships at night.

In 1940, U-boats sank 270 Allied ships in four months. But slowly the Allies gained the upper hand. The U-boats were driven out of the Atlantic by mid-1941 and decisively beaten in March–May 1943. More U-boats appeared in 1945, but they came too late to alter the course of the war.

▲ The crew of two German U-boats take a brief spell on the surface while on patrol in the North Atlantic.

◀ A gunner of a naval destroyer at action stations during a sea battle in the North Atlantic. Naval warships sailed with supply ships to protect them from attack by German submarines.

The *Bismarck* was one of the most feared of all the German warships. When the *Bismarck* sank HMS *Hood* in the Atlantic, four British battleships were sent to the area to track her down. After a fierce battle, the *Bismarck* was crippled by Swordfish torpedo bomber aircraft and pounded by the battleships HMS *King George V* and HMS *Rodney*. More than 2,000 German sailors lost their lives when the *Bismarck* finally went down.

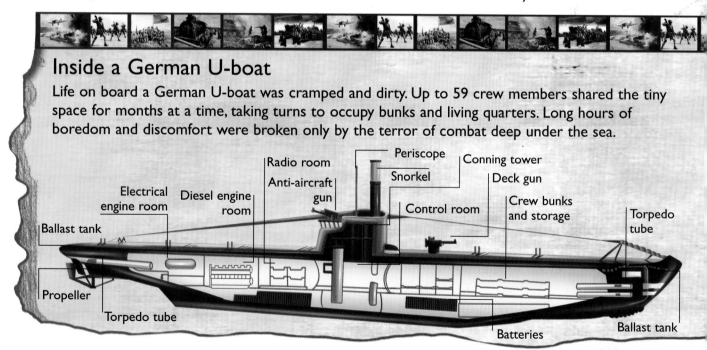

Inside a German U-boat

Life on board a German U-boat was cramped and dirty. Up to 59 crew members shared the tiny space for months at a time, taking turns to occupy bunks and living quarters. Long hours of boredom and discomfort were broken only by the terror of combat deep under the sea.

Radio room

Periscope

Conning tower

Anti-aircraft gun

Snorkel

Deck gun

Electrical engine room

Diesel engine room

Crew bunks and storage

Torpedo tube

Control room

Ballast tank

Propeller

Torpedo tube

Batteries

Ballast tank

War of Words

During the war, both sides used propaganda to win support for their cause and to undermine the enemy.

Nazi propaganda

In Germany, Hitler's information minister Josef Goebbels hired top writers and film directors to spread Nazi ideas. Posters and propaganda films showed heroic soldiers fighting for the 'Fatherland', while women stayed at home to cook and care for children. Jews were shown as evil, sinister people who were responsible for all Germany's problems.

▲ Joseph Goebbels (1897–1945) invented powerful propaganda techniques that are still used by politicians today.

▼ Top-ranking Nazis show their loyalty to Hitler (circled) at a political meeting. Emblems such as the eagle and swastika were deliberately used by Goebbels to make people feel strong and united behind the Nazi leadership.

▲ During the war, the Englishman William Joyce, nicknamed 'Lord Haw-Haw', swapped sides to make propaganda broadcasts for the Nazis. He was later captured by the Allies and executed as a traitor.

The eagle – symbol of the German 'Reich' (empire)

The Nazi swastika

Make a poster

In Britain and America, many posters were produced to encourage people to join the armed forces and to help the war effort in simple ways, such as saving petrol or knitting warm pullovers for soldiers and sailors.

Imagine you are working for the British Ministry of Information. Look at the posters on this page, then see if you can think up your own poster to help the war effort. The example (bottom right) is based on the poster shown below.

▲ This poster was produced in 1942 by the US Navy Recruitment Bureau.

▲ Rationing meant there was not a wide choice of healthy food to eat. This campaign encouraged people to grow fruit and vegetables in their back garden or allotment.

The Secret War

In wartime, countries need to find out all they can about their enemy's strengths and weaknesses – and to keep their own plans as secret as possible. World War II saw many clever and complicated tricks and deceptions.

D-Day deception

In spring 1944, the Allies prepared to launch a massive invasion force across the English Channel to fight Hitler's armies in Europe. The date set for the assault was 6 June 1944, codenamed 'D-Day'. But in order for it to succeed, it was vital to deceive the Germans about where the Allied troops would land.

Fake stories put out by double agents made the Germans expect an attack at the Pas de Calais. The real target was the Normandy beaches. When 'D-Day' came, the Germans were caught off-guard. The deception was so successful that even after the landings had begun, the Germans still believed the real attack would come at Pas de Calais.

▲ This machine, known as an Enigma encoder, was used by the Germans to send all their secret messages. It worked like a computer, changing each letter as it was keyed in. Unknown to the Germans, the Enigma code was broken from 1940 onwards. This gave the Allies a huge secret advantage.

◀ The target and timing of the D-Day landings was one of the best-kept secrets of the war. The Allies even created a 'fake army' of wooden tanks to mislead German planes flying overhead!

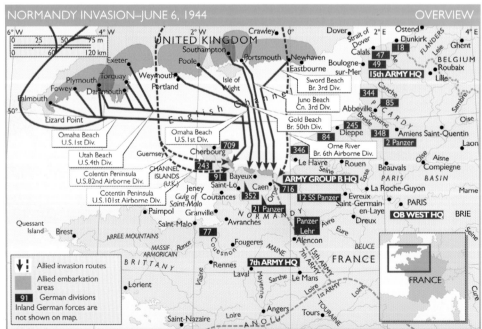

NORMANDY INVASION–JUNE 6, 1944   OVERVIEW

UNITED KINGDOM

Crawley • Dover • Ostend • Dunkirk

Southampton • Portsmouth • Newhaven • Eastbourne • Boulogne-sur-Mer • BELGIUM • Roubaix • Lille

Exeter • Poole • Weymouth • Portland • Isle of Wight

Plymouth • Torquay • Dartmouth • Fowey

Falmouth

Lizard Point

Sword Beach Br. 3rd Div. • Juno Beach Cn. 3rd Div. • Abbeville • Amiens Saint-Quentin

Gold Beach Br. 50th Div. • Dieppe • Laon

Omaha Beach U.S.1st Div. • Omaha Beach U.S.1st Div. • Cherbourg • Orne River Br. 6th Airborne Div. • Le Havre • Rouen • Beauvals • Compiegne • Aisne

Utah Beach U.S.4th Div. • Guernsey • CHANNEL ISLANDS (U.K.) • Bayeux • Caen • ARMY GROUP B HQ • PARIS BASIN • La Roche-Guyon • Marne

Colentin Peninsula U.S.82nd Airborne Div. • Jersey • Saint-Lo • 12 SS Panzer • Evreux • Saint-Germain-en-Laye • PARIS

Cotentin Peninsula U.S.101st Airborne Div. • Gulf of Coutances • Saint-Malo • 21 Panzer • Avranches • Panzer Lehr • Dreux • OB WEST HQ • BRIE

Paimpol • Granville • NORMANDY • Alencon • BEUCE

Quessant Island • Brest • ARREE MOUNTAINS • MASSIF ARMORICAIN • Fougeres • MAINE • FRANCE

BRITTANY • Rennes • 7th ARMY HQ

Laval • Sarthe • Le Mans • FRANCE

Lorient

Saint-Nazaire • Angers • Tours • TOURAINE

Allied invasion routes

Allied embarkation areas

91   German divisions
Inland German forces are not shown on map.

▲ American soldiers wade ashore during the assault on the Normandy beaches. The D-Day landings were the largest naval invasion ever launched, involving almost 100,000 British, American and Canadian troops. Despite heavy casualties, the operation was a success and took the German defenders completely by surprise.

Heroines of the Resistance

In occupied Europe, many Allied secret agents risked their lives working with local resistance fighters to frustrate and undermine the Nazis.

Two of the most famous women agents were Odette Sansom and Violette Szabo. Both were trained in Britain before being dropped by parachute behind enemy lines. After carrying out sabotage missions, Violette Szabo was captured by the Germans and died in a concentration camp. Odette Sansom was betrayed and tortured by the Gestapo, but survived the war.

Both women were later awarded medals for bravery.

◄ Violette Szabo was one of the few women to receive the George Cross, a medal that was specially created to honour acts of outstanding civilian bravery.

Codes and Ciphers

In wartime, spies and special agents had to use codes and ciphers to keep their messages secret from the enemy.

In a code, each letter in a message is replaced with another letter or symbol. A cipher is a special type of code in which letters or numbers are changed using a 'key'. The cipher cannot be broken unless you know the key.

This project shows how to make a code wheel, so you can send secret messages to a friend who has the same code wheel.

Enigma machine

 German wireless operators send and receive secret messages using an Enigma encoding machine. The Enigma settings were changed every day, giving literally millions of possible code combinations.

1

Copy the two code wheels on the facing page onto thick card and cut them out. Make sure you cut around the small black triangle over the letter 'A' on the red inner wheel.

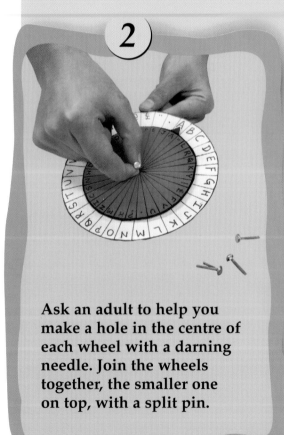

2

Ask an adult to help you make a hole in the centre of each wheel with a darning needle. Join the wheels together, the smaller one on top, with a split pin.

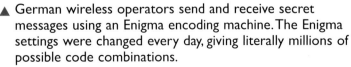

Larger outer wheel

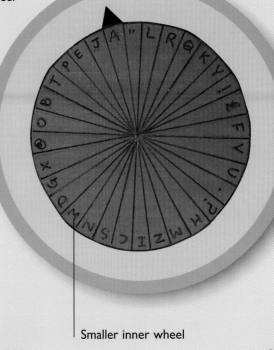

Smaller inner wheel

How to use the code wheel

Here is how to put a message into code so that only a friend with the same code wheel can read it.

1 Write out your message, such as:
   MEET ME AT THE LAKE

2 Choose a character from the wheel to be the key to your cipher – for example, Y. Turn the top wheel until the black triangle points to this letter.

3 Making sure the triangle does not move, find the character for each letter of your message on the outer wheel and write down the letter that is beneath it on the inner wheel.
   BVVA BV JA ATV ?JDV

4 Write the letter key to your code at the front, so your friend can decipher the message.
   YBVVA BVJA ATV ?JDV

5 Don't forget to destroy the original message!

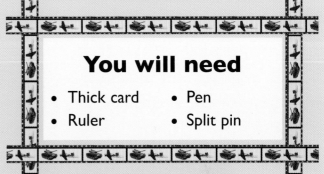

You will need

- Thick card
- Ruler
- Pen
- Split pin

Decoding the message

To read the message, your friend should turn the upper wheel until the black triangle points to the first letter of the message (the key). He or she should then find each character on the inner wheel and write down the letter immediately above it.

The Final Act

In 1945, Russia, Britain and the USA worked together to defeat the Axis powers. In the Pacific, the war ended when the Americans dropped the first atom bomb on the Japanese city of Hiroshima.

Defeat of Hitler

On 25 April, Russian soldiers surrounded the German capital Berlin and slowly pushed into the city. Hitler refused to surrender, forcing the Germans to fight to the end. On 30 April, Russian troops captured the Reichstag, Germany's parliament building. Hitler committed suicide. The new German leader, Admiral Karl Doenitz, ordered a surrender. By 8 May 1945, the war in Europe was over.

The Holocaust

The full horror of the Nazi persecution of the Jews did not become known until the end of the war. From 1934 onwards, millions of men, women and children from all over Europe were deported and killed in Nazi concentration camps. Most of the victims were Jews, but many other groups also suffered. This terrible mass slaughter became known as the Holocaust.

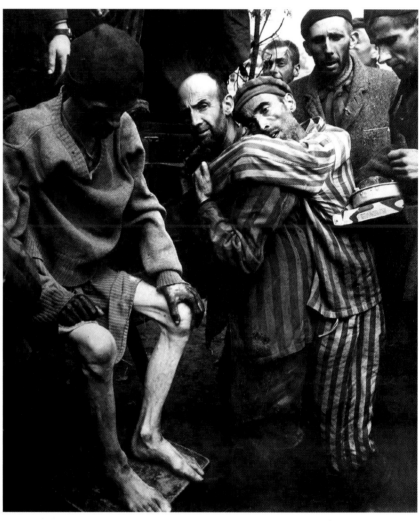

▲ Starving concentration camp survivors wait to be freed by Allied soldiers. In the death camp at Auschwitz in Poland, millions were deliberately killed in specially built gas chambers. Many thousands more died in camps across Europe as a result of cruel treatment and inhuman living conditions.

War in the Pacific

After the Pearl Harbor attack of 1941, Japanese forces swept into Southeast Asia and the southwest Pacific. The Americans struck back at Midway in 1942, and in 1945 fierce battles were fought at Iwo Jima and Okinawa. Finally the dropping of the world's first atomic bomb on Hiroshima on 6 August 1945 (see below) forced the Japanese to surrender.

February 1945: ▶
US marines raise the flag on the island of Iwo Jima. By the time the battle ended, 6,825 US servicemen had died and almost the entire Japanese force of 21,000 men had been destroyed.

The atom bomb

The atom bomb was a terrible weapon which had never been used before. The Americans claimed that the bombs dropped on Hiroshima and Nagasaki actually saved lives by ending the war quickly and avoiding a land battle, but argument about the decision still goes on today.

◀ The huge bombs dropped on Hiroshima and Nagasaki killed approximately 240,000 people. Around half were killed outright. The rest died later of injuries and radiation sickness.

Victory!

After the Germans officially surrendered on 8 May 1945, thousands of people all over Europe poured onto the streets, waving flags and lighting bonfires and fireworks to celebrate. This day became known afterwards as VE or 'Victory in Europe' Day.

In America there were big celebrations on 15 August, when Japanese forces in the Pacific surrendered to General Douglas MacArthur on board the USS *Missouri*.

This project show you how to make victory flags, bunting and medals.

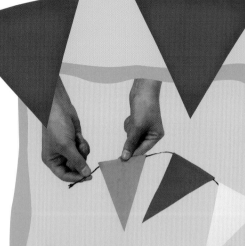

Bunting

Cut triangles out of red, blue and white paper and glue them to a long piece of string.

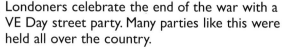

▲ Londoners celebrate the end of the war with a VE Day street party. Many parties like this were held all over the country.

▲ The Burma Star was awarded to British soldiers who served in Burma.

▲ The Red Star was one of the main medals awarded to Soviet (Russian) soldiers.

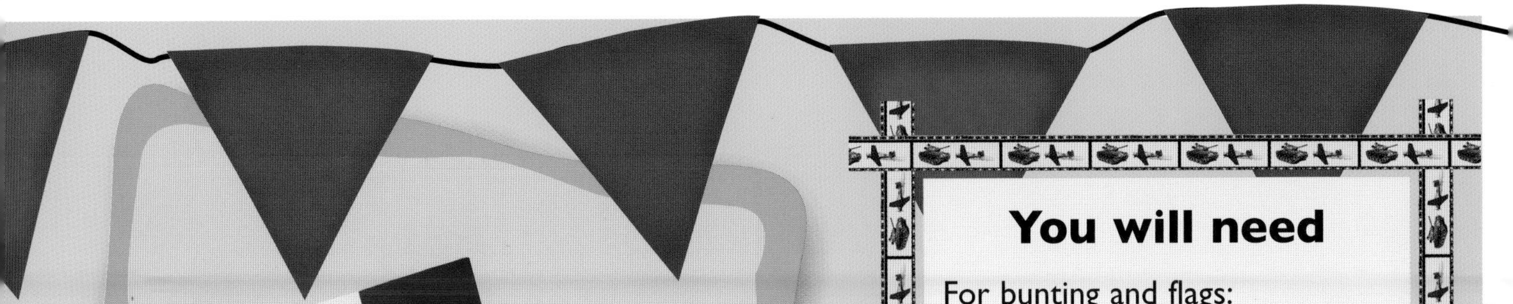

Flags

Draw and colour flag designs on to plain paper measuring 13 x 6 cm. Fold the short left edge back 1 cm and glue onto a lolly stick.

You will need

For bunting and flags:
- Coloured paper
- String
- Glue
- Plain paper
- Coloured pens
- Wooden lolly sticks

For medals:
- Thick card
- Gold and silver foil
- Pen top or pencil
- Black poster paint
- Ribbon
- Glue
- Safety pin

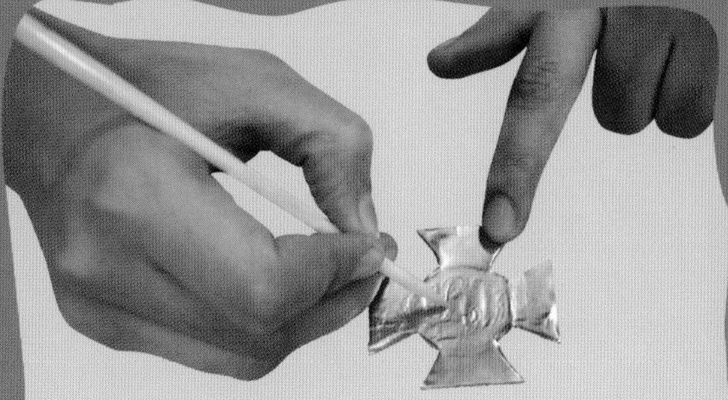

Medals

Cover card circles or star shapes with foil. Engrave a design into the foil with a pen top or pencil. Rub a little black poster paint into the grooves to make the design stand out.

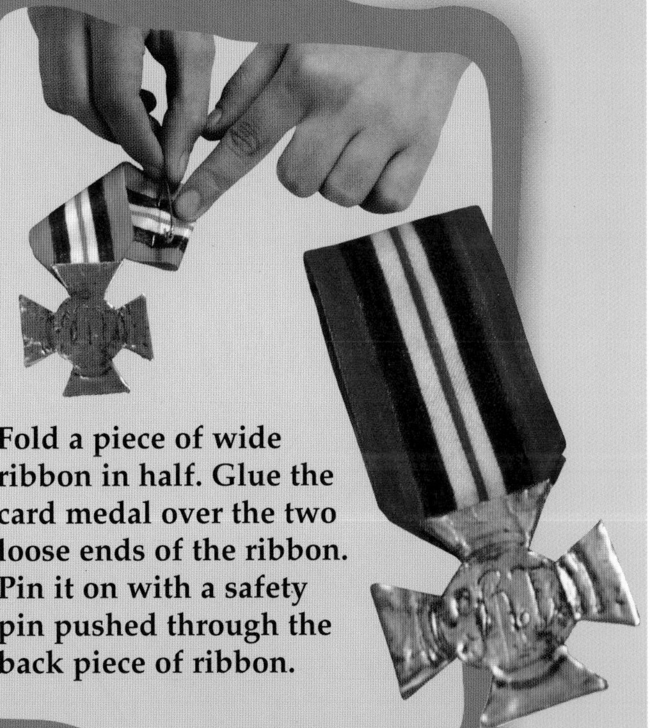

Fold a piece of wide ribbon in half. Glue the card medal over the two loose ends of the ribbon. Pin it on with a safety pin pushed through the back piece of ribbon.

Timeline

19 Aug, 1934 Adolf Hitler becomes Führer of Germany.

1 Sept, 1939 Nazis invade Poland.

3 Sept, 1939 Britain, France, Australia and New Zealand declare war on Germany.

14 June, 1940 Germans enter Paris.

10 July, 1940 Battle of Britain begins.

7 Sept, 1940 German Blitz against England begins.

27 Sept, 1940 Tripartite (Axis) Pact signed by Germany, Italy and Japan.

22 June, 1941 Germany attacks Soviet Union as Operation Barbarossa begins.

12 July, 1941 Mutual Assistance agreement between British and Soviets.

7 Dec, 1941 Japanese bomb Pearl Harbor.

8 Dec, 1941 United States and Britain declare war on Japan.

June, 1942 Mass murder of Jews by gassing begins at Auschwitz.

6 June, 1944 D-Day landings in Normandy.

25 Aug, 1944 Liberation of Paris.

21 April, 1945 Soviets reach Berlin.

30 April, 1945 Adolf Hitler commits suicide.

7 May, 1945 Unconditional surrender of all German forces to Allies.

8 May, 1945 VE (Victory in Europe) Day.

6 Aug, 1945 First atomic bomb dropped, on Hiroshima, Japan.

9 Aug, 1945 Second atomic bomb dropped, on Nagasaki, Japan.

2 Sept, 1945 Japanese sign the surrender agreement; VJ (Victory over Japan) Day.

Glossary

Air raid An attack by enemy planes that drop bombs.

Air-raid shelter An underground shelter where people could escape to stay safe from bombs.

Allies The armies that fought against Germany, Japan and Italy. Included Britain, France, Russia, Canada and USA.

Atom bomb The most powerful bomb developed during WWII that was dropped on Hiroshima and Nagasaki.

Axis The armies of the Germany, Japan and Italy.

Blitz The heavy bombing of the major cities of Britain by the German air force.

Blitzkrieg The invasion of Poland by Hitler's army.

Ciphers Codes used by armies to keep their communications secret.

Civilian A person not in the armed services or the police force.

Concentration camps Camps that were run by Hitler's army where Jews were imprisoned and tortured.

Deception The act of tricking someone into believing something.

Evacuation The process of moving people out of a particular area for their own safety.

Fuselage The main body of an aircraft.

Holocaust The slaughter of millions of Jews by the Nazi army.

Nazi Originally the members of the Nazi party run by Adolf Hitler. Later used to refer to members of the German armed forces.

Propaganda Communications designed to mislead the people through posters, news articles, movies and other media.

Radar A machine used to detect aircraft from far away.

Rationing The practice of dividing the available food items equally among the people.

Torpedo A type of bomb used by the ships at sea.

U-boats Submarines used by the German Navy.

Warship A naval ship.

Index

Webfinder

http://www.bbc.co.uk/history/worldwars/wwtwo/
http://www.bbc.co.uk/history/worldwars/wwtwo/
The BBC's archive of documents and articles relating to the history of the Second World War.

http://www.secondworldwar.co.uk/
http://www.secondworldwar.co.uk/
A general World War Two resource, providing background information and useful and interesting facts.

http://www.world-war-2.info/
http://www.world-war-2.info/
Offers information on World War 2 history, timeline, facts, quotes, pictures, posters, aircraft, weapons, battles, memorials, links, and more.

MAKING HISTORY

SERIES CONTENTS

EGYPT
River kingdom • Pharaohs and priests • Dress like an Egyptian • On the banks of the Nile
Make a shaduf • Living in a town • Make Egyptian jewellery • Friends and family • Play 'Snake'
Writing, counting and discovering • Make a lucky pendant • Everlasting life
Make a mummy mask • Timeline • Glossary
Index and Webfinder

ROME
What do we know about the Romans? • City and people • Dress like a Roman • Army and empire
Make a Roman standard • Brilliant builders • Make a mosaic fish • Friends and families
Play knucklebones • Guardian gods • Make a bulla and lucky charms • Sports and games
Make gladiator weapons • Timeline • Glossary • Index and Webfinder

PIRATES
World of piracy • Caribbean buccaneers • Dress like a pirate • Corsairs and privateers
Make a treasure chest • Pirate ships • Make a pirate flag • Life on board • Make a pirate's fruit salad
Attack at sea • Make a pirate's dagger • Treasure! • Make a treasure map and case
Timeline • Glossary • Index and Webfinder

KNIGHTS
Knights and chivalry • Becoming a knight • Dress like a knight • Clothing and armour
Make a knight's helmet • Weapons • Make a sword and shield • Castles
Play Fox and Geese • Tournaments • Make some pennants • Knightly orders
Make a jewelled chalice • Timeline • Glossary • Index and Webfinder

VICTORIANS
Who were the Victorians? • Queen and country • Make a top hat • Workshop of the world
Make a loom • How to weave • Rich lives, poor lives • Scrapbooking • Fun and games
Victorian Christmas; make some decorations • New inventions, new discoveries • Make a zoetrope
The British Empire • Timeline • Glossary • Index and Webfinder

WORLD WAR TWO
The world at war • Outbreak of war • Food rationing game • War in the skies
Making model planes • The Home Front • Make do and mend (How to make a rag doll)
The war at sea • Propaganda • Dig For Victory • Spies and secret services in World War Two
Spies and spying in World War Two • The end of the war • Victory
Glossary • Index and Webfinder